IN CONGRESS. JULY 4, 1776

The unanimous Declaration of the thirteen united States of America.

When in the Course of human events, it becomes necessary for one people to dissolve the political bands which have connected them with another, and to assume among the powers of the earth, the separate and equal station to which the Laws of Nature and of Nature's God entitle them, a decent respect to the opinions of mankind requires that they should declare the causes which impel them to the separation. — We hold these truths to be self-evident, that all men are created equal, that they are endowed by their Creator with certain unalienable Rights, that among these are Life, Liberty and the pursuit of Happiness. — That to secure these rights, Governments are instituted among Men, deriving their just powers from the consent of the governed, — That whenever any Form of Government becomes destructive of these ends, it is the Right of the People to alter or to abolish it, and to institute new Government, laying its foundation on such principles and organizing its powers in such form, as to them shall seem most likely to effect their Safety and Happiness. Prudence, indeed, will dictate that Governments long established should not be changed for light and transient causes; and accordingly all experience hath shewn, that mankind are more disposed to suffer, while evils are sufferable, than to right themselves by abolishing the forms to which they are accustomed. But when a long train of abuses and usurpations, pursuing invariably the same Object evinces a design to reduce them under absolute Despotism, it is their right, it is their duty, to throw off such Government, and to provide new Guards for their future security. — Such has been the patient sufferance of these Colonies; and such is now the necessity which constrains them to alter their former Systems of Government. The history of the present King of Great Britain is a history of repeated injuries and usurpations, all having in direct object the establishment of an absolute Tyranny over these States. To prove this, let Facts be submitted to a candid world.

He has refused his Assent to Laws, the most wholesome and necessary for the public good.

He has forbidden his Governors to pass Laws of immediate and pressing importance, unless suspended in their operation till his Assent should be obtained; and when so suspended, he has utterly neglected to attend to them.

He has refused to pass other Laws for the accommodation of large districts of people, unless those people would relinquish the right of Representation in the Legislature, a right inestimable to them and formidable to tyrants only.

He has called together legislative bodies at places unusual, uncomfortable, and distant from the depository of their public Records, for the sole purpose of fatiguing them into compliance with his measures.

He has dissolved Representative Houses repeatedly, for opposing with manly firmness his invasions on the rights of the people.

He has refused for a long time, after such dissolutions, to cause others to be elected; whereby the Legislative powers, incapable of Annihilation, have returned to the People at large for their exercise; the State remaining in the mean time exposed to all the dangers of invasion from without, and convulsions within.

He has endeavoured to prevent the population of these States; for that purpose obstructing the Laws for Naturalization of Foreigners; refusing to pass others to encourage their migrations hither, and raising the conditions of new Appropriations of Lands.

He has obstructed the Administration of Justice, by refusing his Assent to Laws for establishing Judiciary powers.

He has made Judges dependent on his Will alone, for the tenure of their offices, and the amount and payment of their salaries.

He has erected a multitude of New Offices, and sent hither swarms of Officers to harrass our people, and eat out their substance.

He has kept among us, in times of peace, Standing Armies without the Consent of our legislatures.

He has affected to render the Military independent of and superior to the Civil power.

He has combined with others to subject us to a jurisdiction foreign to our constitution, and unacknowledged by our laws; giving his Assent to their Acts of pretended Legislation:

For Quartering large bodies of armed troops among us:

For protecting them, by a mock Trial, from punishment for any Murders which they should commit on the Inhabitants of these States:

For cutting off our Trade with all parts of the world:

For imposing Taxes on us without our Consent:

For depriving us in many cases, of the benefits of Trial by jury:

For transporting us beyond Seas to be tried for pretended offences

For abolishing the free System of English Laws in a neighbouring Province, establishing therein an Arbitrary government, and enlarging its Boundaries so as to render it at once an example and fit instrument for introducing the same absolute rule into these Colonies:

For taking away our Charters, abolishing our most valuable Laws, and altering fundamentally the Forms of our Governments:

For suspending our own Legislatures, and declaring themselves invested with power to legislate for us in all cases whatsoever.

He has abdicated Government here, by declaring us out of his Protection and waging War against us.

He has plundered our seas, ravaged our Coasts, burnt our towns, and destroyed the lives of our people.

He is at this time transporting large Armies of foreign Mercenaries to compleat the works of death, desolation and tyranny, already begun with circumstances of Cruelty & perfidy scarcely paralleled in the most barbarous ages, and totally unworthy the Head of a civilized nation.

He has constrained our fellow Citizens taken Captive on the high Seas to bear Arms against their Country, to become the executioners of their friends and Brethren, or to fall themselves by their Hands.

He has excited domestic insurrections amongst us, and has endeavoured to bring on the inhabitants of our frontiers, the merciless Indian Savages, whose known rule of warfare, is an undistinguished destruction of all ages, sexes and conditions.

In every stage of these Oppressions We have Petitioned for Redress in the most humble terms: Our repeated Petitions have been answered only by repeated injury. A Prince whose character is thus marked by every act which may define a Tyrant, is unfit to be the ruler of a free people.

Nor have We been wanting in attentions to our Brittish brethren. We have warned them from time to time of attempts by their legislature to extend an unwarrantable jurisdiction over us. We have reminded them of the circumstances of our emigration and settlement here. We have appealed to their native justice and magnanimity, and we have conjured them by the ties of our common kindred to disavow these usurpations, which would inevitably interrupt our connections and correspondence. They too have been deaf to the voice of justice and of consanguinity. We must, therefore, acquiesce in the necessity, which denounces our Separation, and hold them, as we hold the rest of mankind, Enemies in War, in Peace Friends.

We, therefore, the Representatives of the united States of America, in General Congress, Assembled, appealing to the Supreme Judge of the world for the rectitude of our intentions, do, in the Name, and by Authority of the good People of these Colonies, solemnly publish and declare, That these United Colonies are, and of Right ought to be Free and Independent States; that they are Absolved from all Allegiance to the British Crown, and that all political connection between them and the State of Great Britain, is and ought to be totally dissolved; and that as Free and Independent States, they have full Power to levy War, conclude Peace, contract Alliances, establish Commerce, and to do all other Acts and Things which Independent States may of right do. — And for the support of this Declaration, with a firm reliance on the protection of divine Providence, we mutually pledge to each other our Lives, our Fortunes and our sacred Honor.

John Hancock

Button Gwinnett
Lyman Hall
Geo Walton.

Wm Hooper
Joseph Hewes,
John Penn

Edward Rutledge.

Thos Heyward Junr.
Thomas Lynch Junr.
Arthur Middleton

Samuel Chase
Wm Paca
Thos Stone
Charles Carroll of Carrollton

George Wythe
Richard Henry Lee
Th Jefferson
Benja Harrison
Thos Nelson jr.
Francis Lightfoot Lee
Carter Braxton

Robt Morris
Benjamin Rush
Benja Franklin
John Morton
Geo Clymer
Jas Smith
Geo Taylor
James Wilson
Geo. Ross
Caesar Rodney
Geo Read
Tho M:Kean

Wm Floyd
Phil. Livingston
Frans Lewis
Lewis Morris

Richd Stockton
Jno Witherspoon
Fras Hopkinson
John Hart
Abra Clark

Josiah Bartlett
Wm Whipple
Saml Adams
John Adams
Robt Treat Paine
Elbridge Gerry
Step Hopkins
William Ellery
Roger Sherman
Samel Huntington
Wm Williams
Oliver Wolcott
Matthew Thornton

THE STORY OF THE
DECLARATION of
INDEPENDENCE

By Norman Richards

Illustrations by Tom Dunnington

CHILDRENS PRESS, Chicago

Library of Congress Catalog Card Number: 68-24379

Copyright © 1968, Regensteiner Publishing Enterprises, Inc.
All rights reserved. Printed in the U.S.A.
Published simultaneously in Canada

The Pilgrims landed at Plymouth in 1620.

They were not the first people who had come from Europe to the shores of America. Explorers had come. Men had come looking for gold and other things that would make them rich. But the Pilgrims were the first who came to settle down and make permanent homes in the wilderness.

They were thousands of miles from the king and the government of England. They decided to make their own laws and they agreed to obey them. The Pilgrim men signed a paper that is now called the *Mayflower Compact*. The paper said that each man had the right to vote, and that they could make their own laws and choose their own leaders. Men govern themselves? This was a new and surprising idea. And it worked well for the Pilgrims.

Other colonies were set up along the eastern coast of America. One hundred and thirteen years after the Pilgrims landed there were thirteen colonies. They were all English colonies under the king. But they were separate and had little to do with each other. Many of the colonies borrowed ideas of self-government from the Pilgrims. Some of them had royal governors, but even these were far from the king.

6

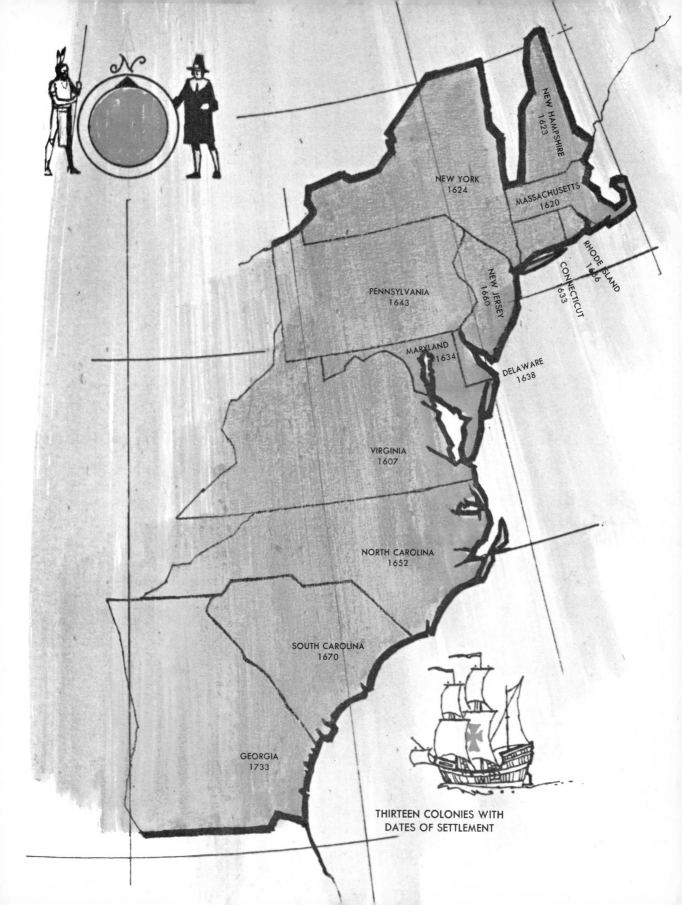

NEW HAMPSHIRE
1623

NEW YORK
1624

MASSACHUSETTS
1620

RHODE ISLAND
1636

CONNECTICUT
1633

PENNSYLVANIA
1643

NEW JERSEY
1660

MARYLAND
1634

DELAWARE
1638

VIRGINIA
1607

NORTH CAROLINA
1652

SOUTH CAROLINA
1670

GEORGIA
1733

THInteen COLONIES WITH
DATES OF SETTLEMENT

Life for the colonists was hard in this strange land. Men had to cut down trees and build houses. They had to dig out the stumps to clear fields where they could grow food. Children worked in the vegetable gardens. They planted the seeds and pulled the weeds. They brought in wood for the fireplaces.

Men made spinning wheels for the wives. The women spun yarn out of flax and cotton. Then they knit or wove the yarn to make cloth for clothes.

The men went hunting for deer, wild turkeys and rabbits for food. Their muskets were important to them. Sometimes unfriendly Indians attacked the colonists. Farmers carried their guns with them when they worked in the fields. Most of them owned land.

For a hundred and thirty-four years after the Pilgrims landed, the king paid no attention to his American colonies. The colonists had stood on their own feet. They had produced what they needed. They had protected themselves from dangers. They had become rugged, independent people.

Some, braver than others, had crossed the mountains to trade for furs with the Indians.

Boston, New York, Philadelphia, Williamsburg were bustling colonial cities. The people were able to buy things from England and other parts of the world. The harbors were crowded with sailing ships. They brought spices, silk and other treasured things from far across the world.

It was about this time that England went to war with France for control of the world. This war spread from India to the heartland of America.

The French had built towns and forts along the St. Lawrence River in Canada, and along the Great Lakes and the Mississippi. England wanted the rich fur trade. She did not want her colonies pinned in along the Atlantic coast.

Fighting went on for almost ten years. There were many Indian uprisings and the colonists suffered in many ways. The French were finally defeated. All of Canada, the Great Lakes region and the upper Mississippi valley belonged to the English.

At last the king thought of his colonies along the coast. He needed money to pay his soldiers and to pay his debts brought on by his long war with France.

King George III of England put a tax on everything the colonists bought. He put a tax on sugar and molasses and other things the colonists needed in their businesses. He forbade them to buy manufactured goods from any country but England.

The independent colonists were angry. They smuggled goods in from other countries.

The king sent warships to cruise along the coast. But there were not enough sailing ships in all England to watch every harbor in America. Smuggled goods kept coming in.

The king sent soldiers into the colonists' homes to search for smuggled goods. The soldiers had slips of paper called *Writs of Assistance*. They showed these slips and then forced their way into the homes. This made the people angry. A young man in Boston, James Otis, went to court and pleaded for the colonists. "A man's house is his castle," he said. "And whilst he is quiet, he is as well guarded as a prince. These writs would destroy what is a basic English liberty." The privacy of the colonists' lives was being destroyed.

But the searches continued.

Some English leaders said to colonial leaders, "Why don't you just pay the taxes and obey the laws passed by parliament?" Parliament was the king's law-making body.

"We are Englishmen, too," said the colonists. "But we have no one to speak for us in the king's parliament. This is taxation without representation. We won't pay these taxes without representation."

Things went from bad to worse over several years. Many things made the colonists mad. They refused to buy tax stamps to put on all their newspapers and other papers. They resented the British soldiers. They did not like having England keep them from manufacturing anything for themselves.

One day there was a skirmish with the British soldiers in Boston and five men were killed.

The British finally took the tax off everything but tea. And there was an uneasy peace for about three years.

Then the British government passed the "Tea Act." The tea was not only taxed but it was sold through agents of the British East India Company. This would put colonial merchants out of business. The British wanted to help the East India Company. They hoped lots of money would come to England.

Ships loaded with tea arrived in America.

Some of the colonies sent the ships back to England. Some put the tea in storehouses and left it there.

In Boston, the governor's family was making a profit out of tea. He refused to give the ships permission to leave the harbor.

"We will throw the tea overboard," said some of the angry colonists.

On a cold December night in 1773 a group of Boston men appeared on the wharves by the gray water. They were dressed as Indians. Their faces were painted. They were grim and angry. They climbed into small boats and rowed out to the anchored ships. They scrambled aboard. War whoops cut through the fog as they ran about the ships.

The men picked up the wooden chests and smashed them open. They threw 342 chests of tea overboard.

When they had finished, the British ships were
surrounded by chests bobbing in the water that was
brown with tea. People called it the *Boston Tea
Party*.

When King George heard about it he was furious. Those American colonists must be forced to live under and obey English laws.

Many red-coated British soldiers were sent to Boston. Their commander, General Gage, lived in the governor's mansion. Boston port was closed to all shipping. Town meetings were not allowed. The people of Boston had to provide living quarters for the British soldiers.

The British military government cut off the colony of Massachusetts from the rest of America. Hopefully the other colonies would be frightened by this punishment of Massachusetts and give no more trouble.

But the people in other colonies became angry instead of afraid. They felt that the people of Boston were right in wanting to vote, choose their own leaders and make their own laws. This was the desire of all the colonists.

With Boston harbor closed, people could not get the food and other supplies they needed. But sud-

denly all kinds of things began to arrive by land from the other colonies.

Herds of cattle were driven over the narrow country roads to Boston. Wagonloads of grain were sent in. Men on horseback brought packets of money to help the people. Cartloads of leather were sent to Boston shoemakers. Cloth was sent from New York and Philadelphia.

Each of the thirteen colonies always had been separate from the others, bound only to the king. Now with the king taking away all rights to govern themselves, they began to unite.

Twelve of the colonies—all but Georgia—chose representatives of the people to meet in Philadelphia. This meeting became known as the *First Continental Congress.*

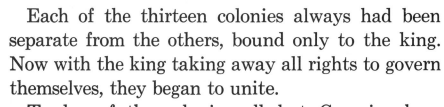

CARPENTERS' HALL

Fifty-six men came to Carpenters' Hall in September of 1774. They talked and worked together for almost two months. They agreed to buy nothing from the British and to sell nothing to them and to use no British goods. They wrote a long list of complaints of the ways they were being treated as English citizens. They sent this to the king.

Before they went home they agreed that if the king paid no attention to their rights—if he did nothing to set things straight—they would meet again on May 10, 1775.

There was no answer from the king and the struggle to resist him became an open fight.

Colonial leaders in Boston such as John Hancock, Samuel Adams and John Adams, urged the people to drive the British out. These men were called *patriots*. They believed so strongly in the right of free men to form their own government that they were willing to fight for it, if necessary.

They were storing guns and ammunition outside the city of Boston. Farmers were ready to pick up their guns and fight the king's troops on a minute's notice. They were called *Minutemen*.

Early in the morning of April 19, 1775, British General Gage sent soldiers marching out from Boston to the village of Concord. He knew that the patriots had stored some ammunition there. He wanted to seize it.

Two horsemen, Paul Revere and William Dawes, rode toward Concord warning the Minutemen that the British were coming.

When the red-coated soldiers reached the town of Lexington on the road to Concord, they met a small group of Minutemen with muskets. Shots were fired and several colonists were killed and others were wounded. The Minutemen retreated and the British marched on to Concord.

The Minutemen had gathered in larger numbers at a small bridge in Concord. A fierce battle took place. The British soldiers had to retreat to Boston. All along the way patriots fired at them from behind trees, bushes and stone walls.

Now the Massachusetts patriots were really furious. And most of the other colonies sent armed men to help them fight the British. They joined Artemas Ward who was commander in chief of the Massachusetts troops.

More than twenty thousand men surrounded Boston and tried to drive the British troops out of the city. They were not a well-trained army. About all they could do was keep the city surrounded and make trouble for the British troops.

Finally a military leader from Virginia took command of the patriot army. His name was George Washington. He knew how to lead an army, and he soon had well-trained officers and men. The British no longer laughed at those "Yankee" troops, as they called the patriots.

Washington finally drove the British from Boston and they sailed away, leaving the people to govern themselves again. The British intended to come back with more troops and force the king's laws on the colonists.

Soon there was scattered fighting between patriots and British soldiers in other colonies, too. Some of the British leaders began to realize that they were fighting rugged, independent men who felt strongly about the right to govern themselves.

It would be necessary, and difficult, for the British to deal with each colony separately. Still King George refused to listen to the colonists' complaints. He insisted that they must obey the British government or be punished.

The colonists were saying, "But why should we be punished by British laws when we are not given the rights of our fellow Englishmen at home?"

In the meantime, the *Second Continental Congress* had been meeting day after day in the Pennsylvania State House in Philadelphia. (This beautiful old meeting hall is now called *Independence Hall*, and it still stands in that city today.)

These men were serious leaders from the colonies. They felt strongly about freedom. They had hoped that vigorous protest and the fighting would make the king understand that he would have to change his mind and let the colonists continue to govern themselves within the British Empire. Many of them at first did not want to break away from Great Britain.

The three Massachusetts patriot leaders, John Hancock, Samuel Adams and John Adams, represented their state. They argued that a war was necessary to free the colonies from Britain. Patrick Henry and Richard Henry Lee from Virginia felt the same way. Others were more careful and did not want to go that far. They argued day after day.

INDEPENDENCE HALL

By the spring of 1776 more and more Americans in every colony began to believe that they must break free from Great Britain. The word *Independence* began to to be heard in cities, small towns and on farms when people gathered to talk. There was already so much fighting going on that they would have to become independent or give up all their freedom and be punished by King George.

The members of the Second Continental Congress voted to organize a navy for the colonies, and they agreed to arm privately owned ships to fight off British warships. They sent a patriot to France to ask for that country's help against the British army and navy. The French government agreed to help the colonies fight for their independence.

The members of the Congress sent word home to their colonies. "Discuss the question of independence and instruct us how to vote." Soon answers came back from the colonies. Each time it was the same. "Vote for independence."

In the town meeting form of government in Massachusetts, each free man over twenty-one years of age could vote for or against independence. Men gathered in little towns and in cities to vote. Each town or city then sent a letter to their representatives in the Congress, saying, "Vote for independence." Every town and city had voted for it.

Ever since the Pilgrims had signed the Mayflower

Compact, Americans had believed that absolute rule was wrong. In Europe kings ruled whether the people wanted them or not. Kings believed that it was their divine right to rule.

Americans had been living as free men, making their own laws for one hundred and fifty years. They would never surrender this precious freedom.

Richard Henry Lee of Virginia said in the Continental Congress: "These United Colonies are, and of right ought to be, free and independent states."

The members of the Continental Congress saw now that it was their duty to follow the people's wishes and declare the American colonies independent. They wanted officially to tell the world about the new union of the thirteen United States of America. They also wanted to tell the world why they were breaking away from Great Britain. Five men were chosen to work on the document—John Adams, Thomas Jefferson, Benjamin Franklin, Robert Livingston and Roger Sherman.

They chose young Thomas Jefferson from Virginia to write this official declaration. He was a smart man,

27

and he could express ideas clearly. And they wanted this declaration understood by everybody.

Thomas Jefferson worked for two weeks writing the declaration. He stood at a desk in the second-floor parlor of a house belonging to a Philadelphia bricklayer whom he knew. He wrote on large paper with a quill (a feather) dipped in ink. He would study the sentences he had written the day before. If he didn't like them he would cross them out and write them again.

Jefferson, with four other men, was to present the declaration to the members of the Congress. When he had finished writing the declaration he showed it to John Adams, Benjamin Franklin and the other members of the committee, and they made a few changes.

The Declaration of Independence has two main parts. The first part explains the beliefs of Americans about democracy. It tells that men have certain rights that can't be taken away from them. The signers declared these seven truths to be understood by everyone:

1. That all men are created equal.
2. That all men are born with rights that no one can take away from them.
3. That some of these rights are *life*, *liberty*, and the *right to try to be happy*. (Pursuit of happiness.)

4. That the purpose of a government is to *preserve* these rights for all men.

5. That the government is the servant of the people and gets its powers with the *permission* of the people it governs.

6. That if a government fails to protect people's rights, men have the *right* and the *duty* to change government.

7. That men have the right to form *new* governments that will protect their rights and provide safety and happiness.

The second part of the Declaration of Independence tells how the king refused to grant these rights to Americans. It contains a long list of examples of tyranny by the king. It tells the world why the colonies broke away from his rule and became the United States of America.

This document was presented to the members of the Congress. They debated about it for almost three days. It was approved on July 4, 1776, although the New York delegates did not accept it until eleven days later.

When the Declaration was read aloud from the yard of Independence Hall, on July 8, the crowds of people went wild. They cheered and set off gunpowder explosions. Soldiers marched in a parade and people sang. High in the tower of Independence Hall the great iron bell tolled so that the whole city could hear. It came to be known as the *Liberty Bell.*

The parchment copy of the Declaration was signed by fifty members of the congress on August 2. Six others signed it later.

Several more years of war took place before the Americans finally defeated the British troops and the British decided to quit the war. It was a long, discouraging struggle. General George Washington led the American armies and was the victor when the British surrendered to end the war. The grateful American people elected Washington as their first President, and he is known today as the *Father of His Country.*

Visitors come from all over the world today to see the original piece of paper, the Declaration of Independence, at the National Archives Building in Washington, D.C. The ideas in it have appealed to people in many countries all over the world. They understand the simple principles about the rights of men, and they look to these rights with hope for all mankind. Wherever people value freedom, they remember America's wonderful Declaration of Independence. Americans celebrate Independence Day on the Fourth of July.

About the author: Norman Richards grew up in a small New England town and developed an early interest in history. Among other books that he has written are *The Story of Old Ironsides* and *The Story of the Mayflower Compact*, both of which are in the "Cornerstones of Freedom" series. A graduate of Boston University's School of Journalism, Mr. Richards has written more than a hundred articles on aviation and travel. As managing editor of *Mainliner*, United Air Lines' magazine for passengers, he travels 100,000 miles a year in jets, light planes, and helicopters to cover stories.

About the illustrator: Tom Dunnington grew up in Iowa and Minnesota. He began his art training in Indiana and continued it at the Art Institute and the American Academy of Art in Chicago. He has five children, lives in Elmhurst, west of Chicago, and works full time as a free-lance artist.

THE MINUTEMAN OF CONCORD
BY DANIEL CHESTER FRENCH